SNAKES

MARY HOFF

CREATIVE EDUCATION

THE WILD WORLD OF ANIMALS

Published by Creative Education, 123 South Broad Street, Mankato, Minnesota 56001. Creative Education is an imprint of The Creative Company. Designed by Rita Marshall. Production design by Advertising and Design. Photographs by Alamy (ACE STOCK LIMITED, blickwinkel, BRUCE COLEMAN INC., adrian davies, Danita Delimont, adam eastland, Steven Haggard, Martin Harvey, Peter Arnold, Inc., The Photolibrary Wales, Stock Connection Distribution, David Wall) Getty Images (Theo Allofs, JH Pete Carmichael, David Noton Photography, Matias Klum, Tim Laman, Claus Meyer, Heinrich van den Berg). Copyright © 2007 Creative Education. International copyright reserved in all countries. No part of this book may be reproduced in any form without written permission from the publisher. Printed in the United States of America. Library of Congress Cataloging-in-Publication Data: Hoff, Mary King. Snakes / by Mary Hoff. p. cm. — (The wild world of animals). Includes bibliographical references. ISBN-13: 978-1-58341-436-1. 1. Snakes—Juvenile literature. I. Title. II. Wild world of animals (Creative Education) 2006 597.96—dc22 2005048228. First edition 9 8 7 6 5 4 3 2 1

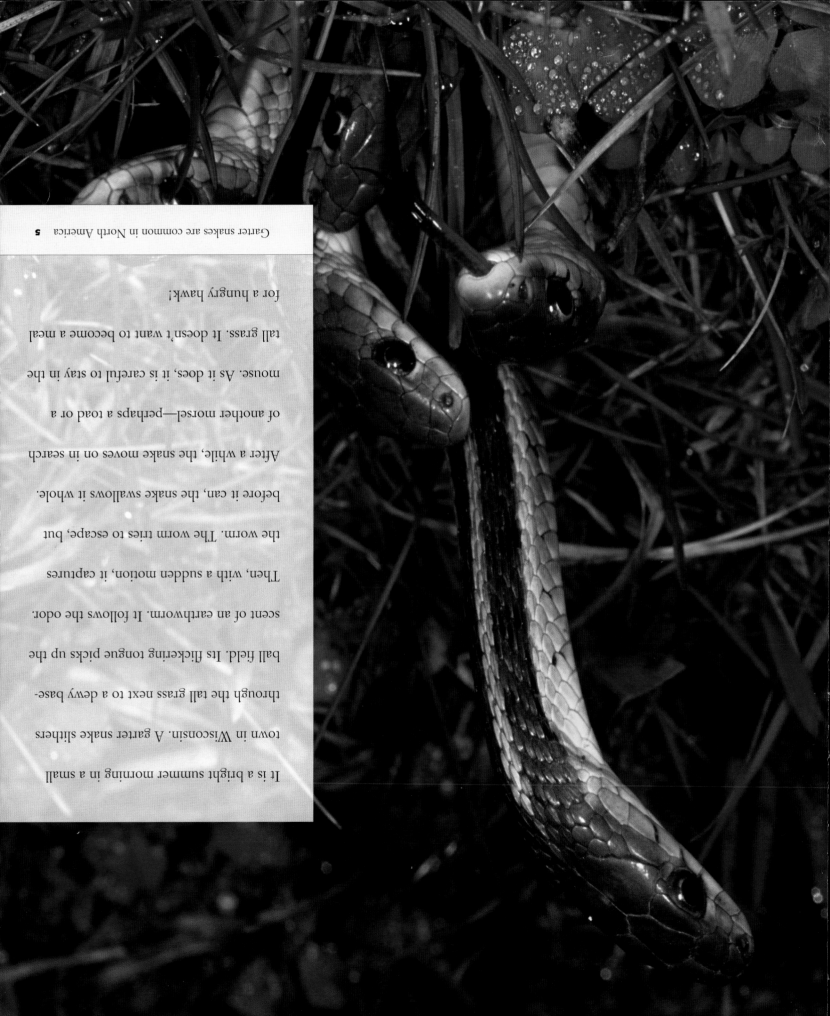

It is a bright summer morning in a small town in Wisconsin. A garter snake slithers through the tall grass next to a dewy base-ball field. Its flickering tongue picks up the scent of an earthworm. It follows the odor.

Then, with a sudden motion, it captures the worm. The worm tries to escape, but before it can, the snake swallows it whole. After a while, the snake moves on in search of another morsel—perhaps a toad or a mouse. As it does, it is careful to stay in the tall grass. It doesn't want to become a meal for a hungry hawk!

SLITHERY AND SCALY

Long and legless, flexible enough to tie themselves into a knot, snakes are fascinating **reptiles**. They are found around the world—in deserts, swamps, forests, prairies, and even lakes and rivers. The only areas where snakes do not live are very cold places, such as Antarctica, and some islands, such as Ireland and New Zealand. Depending on where they live, snakes share their homes with such animals as frogs, fish, gazelles, and foxes.

There are about 2,700 **species** of snakes in the world. They come in many colors, from dull brown to bright red, yellow, and black. Dull or green colors help snakes hide in their **habitat**. Bright colors may warn **predators** that a snake is poisonous or tastes bad.

Different snakes are different sizes. The largest snake ever recorded was a reticulated python from Indonesia. It was about 33 feet (10 m) long. The tiny thread snake, found in the West Indies, is only about as long as a stretched-out paper clip.

8 Pythons are among the world's longest snakes

Snakes are covered by a scaly skin. Their scales are made out of a tough material called keratin, which also makes up human finger-nails. The scales help snakes grip the ground as they crawl. They also make it easy for snakes to bend and stretch as they move.

Big snakes have thousands of scales **9**

Snakes eat many kinds of animals, including frogs, mice, other snakes, birds, and rabbits. Some large snakes even eat monkeys or deer. Snakes have many **adaptations** to help them find, capture, and eat their **prey.** Some snakes have pits in their head that sense the heat live animals give off. Snakes can also feel vibrations through the ground as other animals move around.

10 Many snakes, such as this tree snake, eat lizards

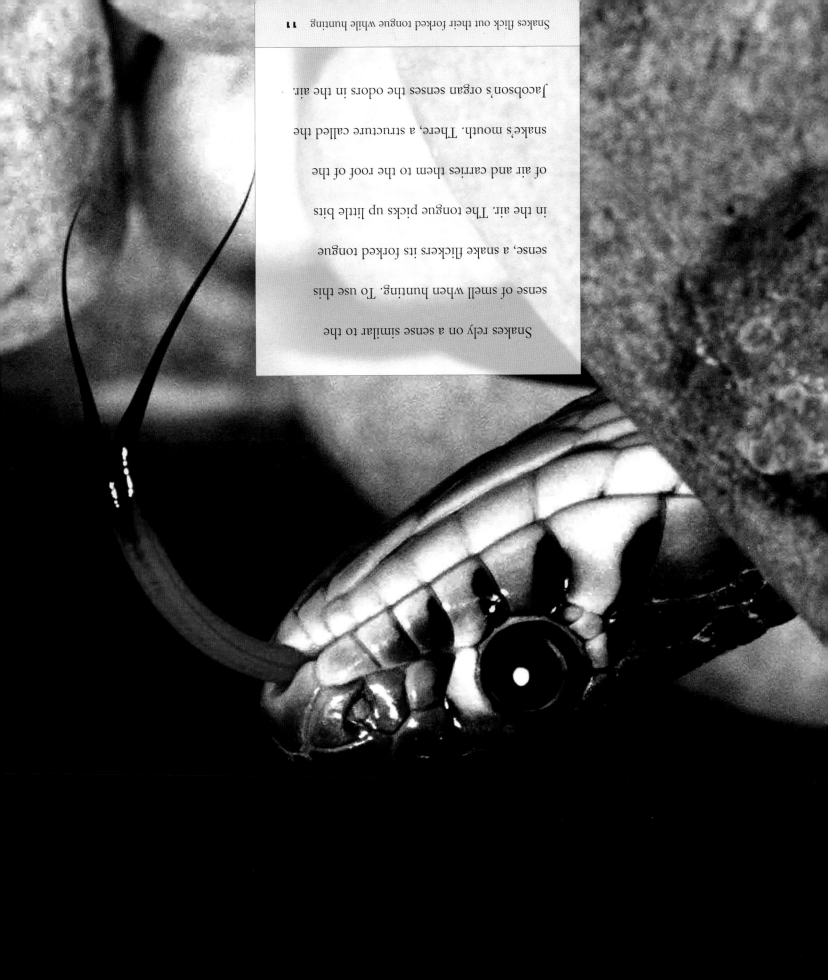

Snakes rely on a sense similar to the sense of smell when hunting. To use this sense, a snake flickers its forked tongue in the air. The tongue picks up little bits of air and carries them to the roof of the snake's mouth. There, a structure called the Jacobson's organ senses the odors in the air.

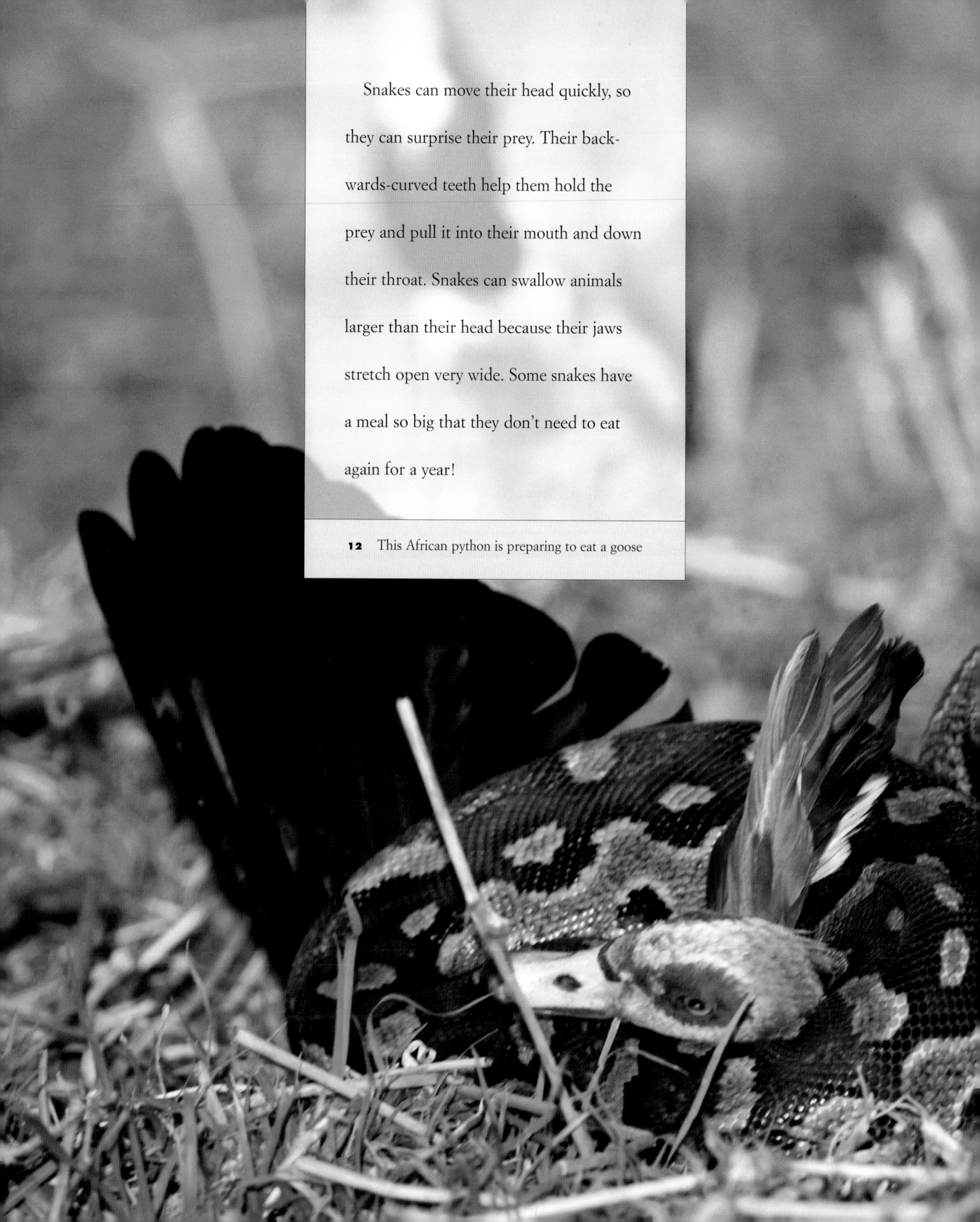

Snakes can move their head quickly, so they can surprise their prey. Their backwards-curved teeth help them hold the prey and pull it into their mouth and down their throat. Snakes can swallow animals larger than their head because their jaws stretch open very wide. Some snakes have a meal so big that they don't need to eat again for a year!

12 This African python is preparing to eat a goose

LIFE AS A SNAKE

Most snakes begin life inside an egg. A female snake usually lays 10 to 40 eggs at a time, although Indian pythons may lay up to 100 eggs. Snake eggs feel like soft leather. They expand as the snake inside of them grows. Some kinds of snakes, such as rattlesnakes and garter snakes, do not lay eggs. Instead, they give birth to live young.

Adult snakes do not take care of their young after they hatch or are born. The little snakes are on their own. They have to figure out how to catch food and hide from hungry predators.

As the little snakes grow, their skin wears out. After a while, they molt, crawling out of their worn-out skin and leaving it inside out in a pile behind them. Snakes continue to molt throughout their lives. They molt most often during their first year, while they are growing rapidly.

Because they are reptiles, snakes need to control their body temperature by moving around. If they are cold, they move to a sunny spot to warm themselves. If they are hot, they find cool shade beneath rocks or behind buildings.

Snakes soak up the sun when the weather is cool **17**

Many snakes get around by wiggling
their body back and forth like a wave.
Some snakes also move by folding and
then stretching their body like an accor-
dion. Other ways of moving include creep-
ing—inching forward in a straight line—
and **sidewinding.**

Snakes spend most of their time hang-
ing out or looking for food. When they
find food, some snakes swallow their
prey alive. Others **suffocate** their prey by
squeezing it. Some snakes are venomous.
They have structures in their head that
make a deadly substance called venom.
When they grab their prey, they inject the
venom with their front teeth, called fangs.
The venom either kills their prey or takes
away its ability to move.

Snakes have enemies, too. Depending on where they live, they have to look out for dogs, cats, eagles, owls, foxes, skunks, and even other snakes. Some snakes use **camouflage to protect themselves from enemies.** Others hiss or puff up their heads to make themselves look scary. Some play dead or give off a stinky substance when they are threatened. Venomous snakes may use their venom on enemies as well as on prey.

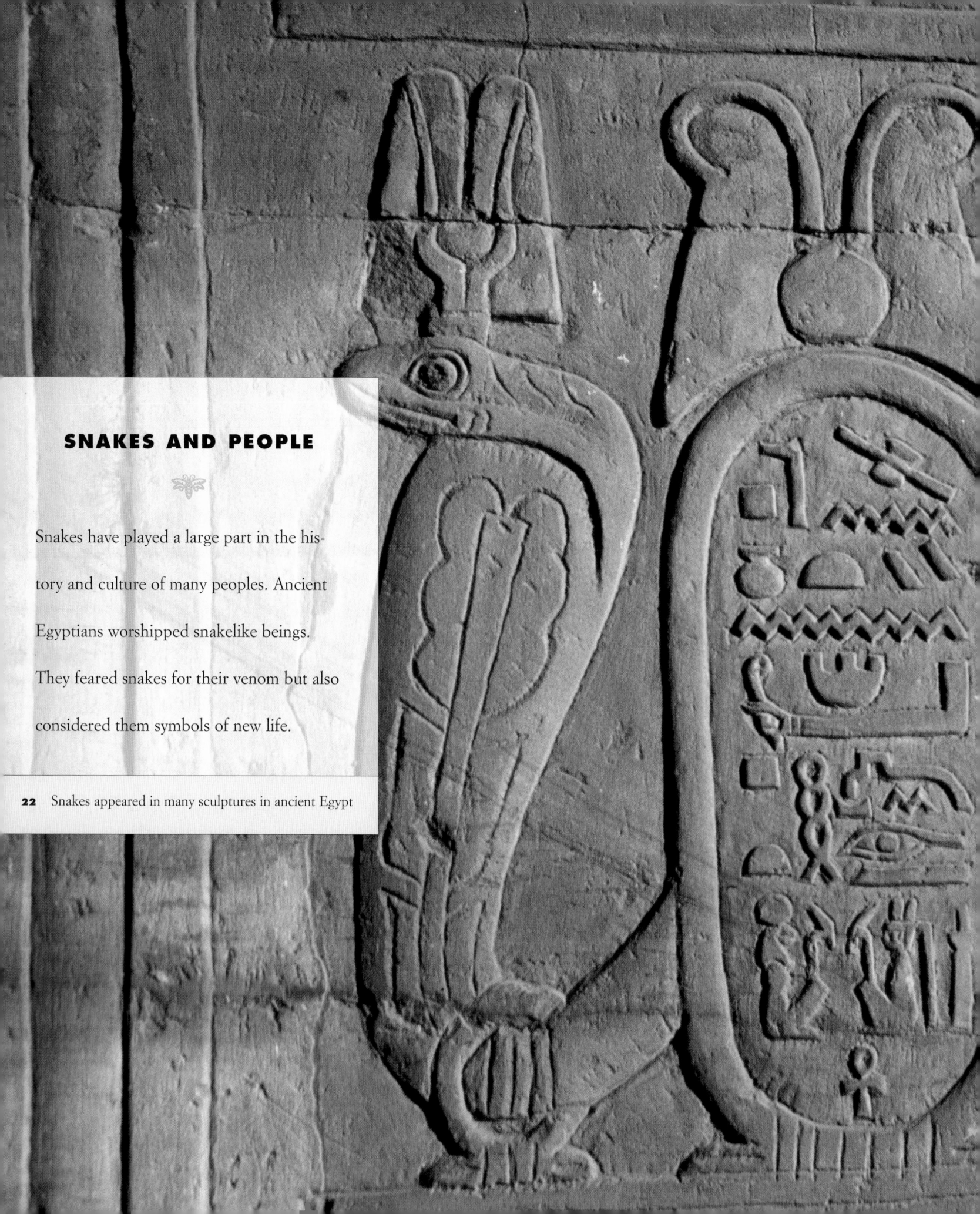

SNAKES AND PEOPLE

Snakes have played a large part in the history and culture of many peoples. Ancient Egyptians worshipped snakelike beings. They feared snakes for their venom but also considered them symbols of new life.

22   Snakes appeared in many sculptures in ancient Egypt

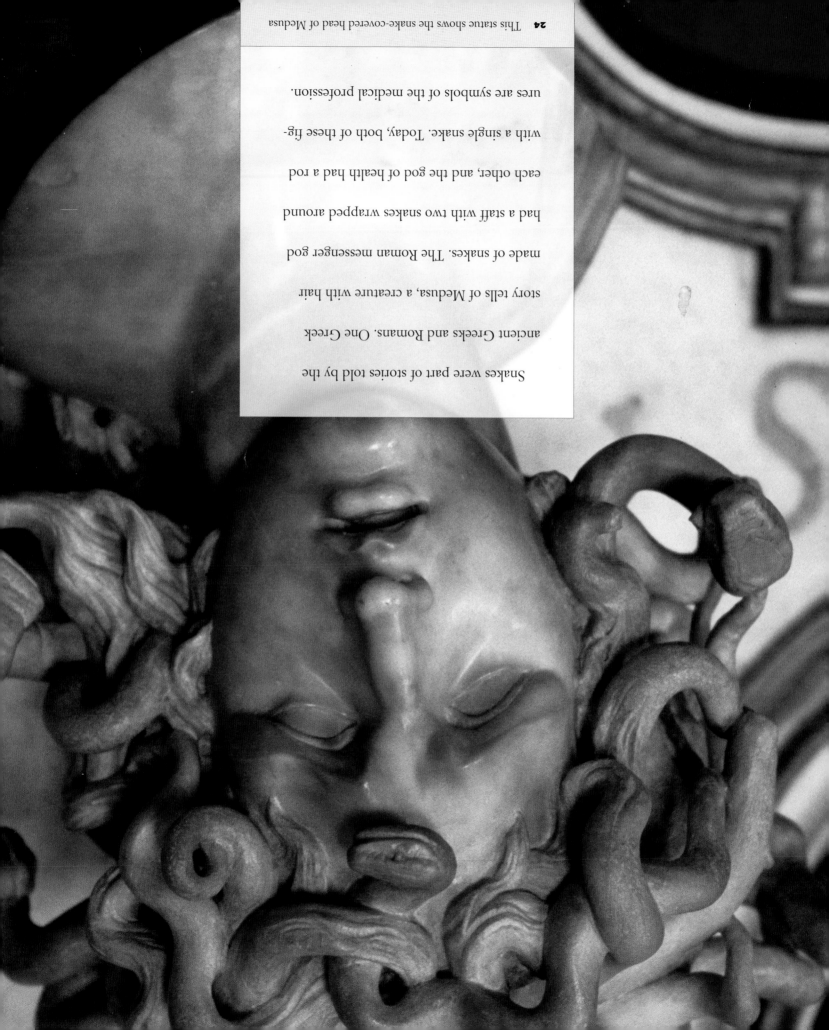

Snakes were part of stories told by the ancient Greeks and Romans. One Greek story tells of Medusa, a creature with hair made of snakes. The Roman messenger god had a staff with two snakes wrapped around each other, and the god of health had a rod with a single snake. Today, both of these figures are symbols of the medical profession.

In Australia, snakes have long been a part of the culture and religion of the **Aborigine** people. A being known as the Rainbow Snake is said to be a symbol of new life. Many African and American Indian stories handed down from generation to generation include snakes, and some American Indian dances involve snakes.

Rainbow snakes live in watery areas and like to swim **25**

In India, some people celebrate a festival that honors a cobra snake god. Snake charmers entertain audiences with live snakes as part of the festival. The snake is one of the animals of the Chinese zodiac, which says that people born in certain years are like certain animals. People born in the year of the snake are said to be wise, charming, and selfish.

Snake charmers are skilled at making cobras calm

Many people dislike snakes. Some venomous snakes, such as the death adder of Australia, can kill a person with a single bite. But most snakes are completely harmless to humans.

Snakes can even be helpful to people.

They eat rodents that harm crops or carry

diseases. They are also food for some peo-

ple. Other people use snakeskin to make

purses and belts. Scientists have used snake

venom to develop medicines for health

problems such as high blood pressure.

Snakes have even been used to study the

effect of gravity on blood flow to help keep

humans healthy while traveling in space.

Snakes face many threats from humans today. Sometimes snakes are run over by cars as they try to cross roads. Other snakes are threatened by the loss of their habitat. Today, more than 200 species of snakes are **endangered** or threatened. Many people are helping to protect these snakes and the places they live to prevent them from becoming **extinct**. By valuing snakes today, people are ensuring that these fascinating reptiles will continue to thrive tomorrow.

GLOSSARY

Aborigine people are dark-skinned, native people of Australia.

Adaptations are features of a living thing that help it survive where it lives.

Camouflage is coloring that helps make an animal hard to see in its surroundings.

An **endangered** animal is one that is at risk of dying off so that it no longer exists on Earth.

When the last of a certain kind of plant or animal dies, we say it has become **extinct**.

The place where a creature lives is called its **habitat**.

Predators are animals that kill and eat other animals.

Prey animals are animals that are caught and eaten by other animals.

Snakes, lizards, turtles, and crocodiles are all **reptiles**. Reptiles are cold-blooded and have scaly skin.

When a snake is **sidewinding**, it lifts part of its body up, then puts it back down in the direction it's traveling.

Some animals are divided into different kinds, or **species**. Members of a species can have young together.

When snakes **suffocate** an animal, they kill it by preventing it from breathing.

BOOKS

Clarke, Penny. *Scary Creatures: Snakes Alive.* Danbury, Conn.: Franklin Watts, 2002.

Markle, Sandra. *Outside and Inside Snakes.* New York: Scholastic, 1995.

Stone, Lynn. *The Wild World of Snakes.* Vero Beach, Fla.: The Rourke Book Company, 2001.

WEB SITES

eNature: Field Guides http://www.enature.com/fieldguides/view_default.asp?curGroupID=7&shapeID=1060

Singapore Zoological Gardens http://www.szgdocent.org/resource/rr/c-main.htm

World Almanac for Kids: Snakes http://www.worldalmanacforkids.com/explore/animals/snake.html

INDEX

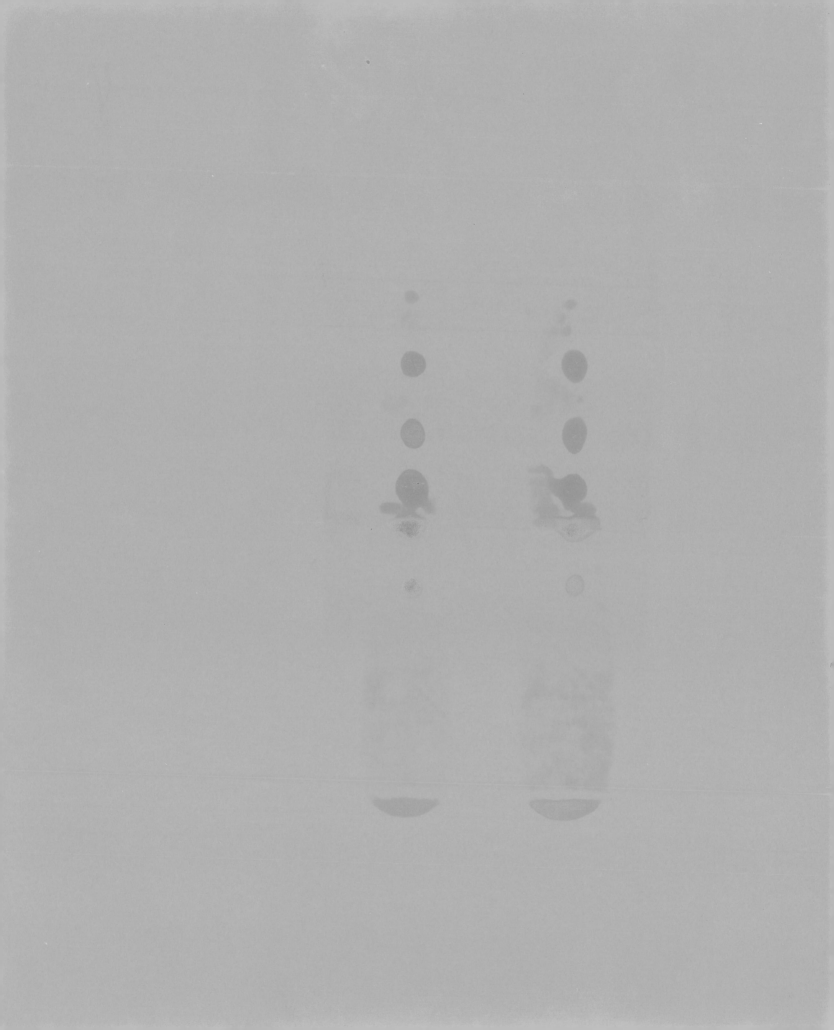